SECU

GRANT MONEY

-Step-by-Step Guide

For

First-Time Homebuyers-

C.R. Wesley

MACRO INVESTMENTS
LLC
S I M P L Y   V A L U E

i

Securing Grants : Step-by-Step Guide For First-Time Homebuyers

Copyright © 2019 by C.R. Wesley.

For information contact :

(info@macroinvestmentsllc.com, http://www.macroinvestmentsllc.com)

Book and Cover design by Designer

ISBN: 9781688447226

First Edition: September 2019

TABLE OF CONTENTS

Introduction

Welcome and good job seeking the knowledge to build wealth. We are happy to help you outline the steps you'll need to take in making your first home purchase. The best part is, you may qualify for grants, or forgivable loans! This literature will help you acquire your first piece of real estate with grants! Follow along with us in this step-by-step guide to give you the necessary information to obtain your grants in your county.

Buying a home is likely to be the most important financial transaction you'll make in your lifetime. If you're seeking to become a homeowner, you'll likely be considering financing the purchase with a mortgage. Being a first-time homebuyer doesn't mean you haven't owned your own home before. It could also mean you haven't owned a home in about three years. Buying a home can be a daunting task, but millions of people have had this encounter and have been successful. If you do your homework, you'll buy a home you can afford while also obtaining down payment assistance.

This down payment assistance is a forgivable loan also known as a down payment assistance grant. We will guide you in completing the right tasks to acquire the grant (or grants) you're seeking. Securing Grants For First-Time Homebuyers by C.R. Wesley has comprised a list of 13 steps you must consider for making your purchase. These steps will illustrate what actions you'll need to take in oder to find, apply, secure your grants and prepare for the home purchasing process.

NOTICE

Throughout the literature, you will see – **(TASK)** – This is where you need to take action and complete these. Completing them will effectively prepare you for the journey you are about to take. A Summary checklist of the tasks is provided. Let's get started!

Chapter 1 – Preparation

Stability

Congratulations! You're motivated to take steps toward your financial freedom! However, before you click through pages of online listings or fall in love with your dream home, you need to do a serious audit of your finances. The first factor is stability in your workplace, meaning that you have a steady source of income. However, if you are self-employed, you have to ensure that you make proper documentation of your revenue and taxes so that you can prove your financial stability. The last thing you would want is to be caught unprepared when it's time for the mortgage payments!

To determine your financial stability, you also have to look at your savings. **(TASK)** It is advisable that you have an emergency savings account with up to three to six months of living expenses. This is aside the amount that would go towards your appraisal, home inspection, attorney fee, earnest money and possible loan origination fees. The grant or grants you'll receive will only cover the down payment.

You should also consider how much you spend every month and where it's going. Costs like food, utilities, kids' activities, clothing, car maintenance, car payments, entertainment, retirement savings, regular savings, and other miscellaneous expenses, are all costs you need to evaluate. Please compute your expenses. **(TASK)** With this information, you will know how much you can afford to allocate to a mortgage payment.

Other factors to consider when determining your stability is the desired location of your new home. How much is the cost of transportation to and from work? This takes into consideration public transportation, your vehicle type, car payments, miles traveled, gas, and other factors that help to estimate the cost of a potential commute. Take time to gather these factors so you know your budget compared to your true finances. **(TASK)** Many things get revealed when you take a closer look at your spending habits. This is an important first step before anything else.

Motivation

I haven't met anyone who didn't desire to own their own home. However, I have met people who owned a home to their peril. You need to discover the motivation behind your desire and decision to buy a home. Don't just buy a home because everybody is doing it. They're actually not. Don't just buy a home because your dad told you that it's silly to "throw money away" on rent because he's also wrong. If you're not prepared for a home, renting is perfect until you're ready. You also shouldn't buy a home because of low mortgage rates or because it's a buyer's market. Your strongest motivation for buying a home should be because you are financially prepared and you want to be a homeowner. Buy a home because you want to settle down and need a place to live for at least five years. Above all, buy a home because you have the financial capability to maintain your property. If other reasons are in place, but this is missing, you may truly own a home but struggle from that time onward. Take in consideration, some of you may save substantially by paying a mortgage depending on your current cost of rent per month. Owning a home is not always more expensive than your current living expenses. Don't worry, we'll get into the numbers.

Don't rush into homeownership because you see it as a measure of adulthood and financial responsibility. It is a huge commitment to own a home, and while it may not even guarantee good investment, it is always a load of work.

Don't let homeownership make a wreck of your finances. Sustainable motivation is one that continues to exist in the face of reality, and the reality about homeownership is that it is not always the creative paradise that remodeling shows make it out to be.

Be ready to own a home such that when you make the purchase, you are improving the quality of your life and reducing its struggles, not the other way around.

Credit

Note: In this section we will refer to many interactions with the lender. This is for information purposes. You will attend a first-time homebuyers class before you select a specific lender. This lender will apply for the grants on your behalf. The topics of preparing your credit involves general lender feedback. These are general inquiries that you can consult with any lender on. So, some inquiries will be general for any lender, and later we will cover lender follow-ups that are specific to the team you'll build.

Credit is very important as it depicts your ability to hold yourself accountable. Primarily, most of the information on your credit report is regarded as debts when comparing your debt to income ratio. It is your responsibility to ask your lender about the debts from your credit report that are considered for this ratio. Make it a point, from this time forward, to minimize the amount of times your credit is pulled by lenders or third parties, specifically "hard pulls". If your credit report is pulled too often it may affect your score negatively. For self-awareness purposes only, you can mitigate this by pulling your credit report yourself. This will enable you to correct anything on your report that is inaccurate. If you find anything that is inaccurate, follow the dispute directions with each credit bureau accordingly. This can possibly increase your score. When you run your own credit, it does not lower your score, and this is considered a "soft pull." A "hard pull" lowers your credit score usually by 3-5 points. Creditors can also run "soft pulls" so, simply ask the creditor whether the report will be a soft pull or hard pull when your credit report has been requested.

You can run your credit for free yearly, to ensure accuracy, at www.annualcreditreport.com. **(TASK)** For future reference, feel free to ask any creditor if they will be doing a soft pull or a hard pull of your credit.

Aside from the fact that many realtors will not spend time with clients that haven't clarified how much they can afford to spend, you must be prepared to make sure your credit rating is as high as possible prior to your application for a mortgage. In most instances, sellers will not even consider an offer if it isn't accompanied with a mortgage pre-approval. A pre-approval means you already passed the lenders' approval process and therefore are guaranteed to be immediately granted the loan up to your eligible limit that you apply for. Since it's unlikely that you have all cash to pay for your home, the next step is to ensure your credit will help you to qualify for a mortgage. With higher credit ratings, you will receive better financing rates, which translates to lower mortgage payments. Overall, to know how your credit score influences your mortgage, you should compare your available credit to your credit use. A credit score is good if you use less than half of your available credit, but your score will be better if you are using less than 30% of your credit ability and top tier if you are using less than 10%. You can learn more about this at www.creditkarma.com. **(TASK)**

Eligibility

Examine Your Debt-to-Income Ratio

Down payment assistance programs usually have lower debt-to-income ratios compared to a typical lender. This helps to prevent the homebuyer from becoming over-extended and also prevents future foreclosure.

For example, a typical down payment assistance program has a ratio of 32/41.

- ✓ In this case, the 32 shows the maximum allowable housing-related debt including principal, taxes, interest, Home Owner Association (HOA) fees, insurance, etc...

- ✓ While 41 shows the maximum allowable percentage of all the recurring debt including credit cards, car payments, school loans etc... At times, a lender may have higher ratios, thereby allowing a back-end ratio of up to 45 percent. Consult with your lender for details.

<u>Income</u>

The income requirement assures lenders that you have the stability to keep repaying the loan in the long term. Lenders will need to confirm your income before making the loan available to you. To prove your worthiness, gather your tax returns for the last two years, the most recent pay stubs, and your bank statements for the past three months **(TASK)**. If you receive alimony or child support by court order, bring the bank verification and orders that your ex-spouse is current on all payments and regularly makes them. This is also included in your income. To qualify for down payment assistance there are income requirements. Your income cannot exceed a particular level per household. This limit is usually the median income for the area you are purchasing in and is deemed by the county. Debt to income qualification requirements can be confirmed with your lender. Be sure to seek the debt to income qualifications out with your lender so you are aware. **(TASK)**

Since you've evaluated your finances, go ahead and see how much house you can buy with the monthly expense that is affordable to you.Go online and use a mortgage calculator to plug in a few example mortgage amounts to see what the monthly payments would be. Let's use a calculator that incorporates taxes and insurance. It's better to have the taxes and insurance factored into your mortgage payment so you don't get behind on taxes. Mortgage accounts with this feature have an escrow account. Use a 30 year fixed rate mortgage as your base plan.

- Here is a link to reference for the mortgage calculator. https://www.nerdwallet.com/mortgages/mortgage-calculator/calculate-mortgage-payment

Attending First Time Homebuyers Class - Getting The Certificate

When you are sure that you meet the income eligibility to qualify for grants, you'll need to find a class to attend that will enlighten you on first-time homebuying. In the U.S., homeownership is among the fastest ways to create generational wealth, and it also helps to strengthen communities. These classes share sufficient information necessary to make an informed decision by prospective homeowners. The topics

covered in these courses include information about eligible grants, the mortgage process, credit, budgeting, insurance, home inspections, working with a real estate agent, a lender, an attorney, an accountant and closing the deal. Most importantly, you'll obtain a certificate of course completion that is usually acceptable for 6 months. This certificate is needed and confirms your eligibility when you apply for any grant programs related to eligible first-time homebuyers. Be sure to choose the class that fits your situation as there are programs about, 1) financial/down payment assistance and 2) programs targeted at individuals with low credit scores. Most times, both topics are covered in one class. Seek out all programs so that you are well-informed. Also confirm the class topics so you are certain you are planning to attend a class you need based upon your grant application plan. **(TASK)**

- ✓ Here is an example from Cook County Illinois' site directing you to a first-time homebuyers class. https://www.chicago.gov/city/en/depts/mayor/supp_inf o/ho_me_buyer_program.html

- ✓ Please complete a google search for " first-time homebuyer classes near me." Be sure to verify the class issues the certificate of completion. The certificate is what qualifies your application for any grant you pursue. Use your county as a resource for the approved classes. This will help confirm you attend a class that issues the certificate, but still ask. **(TASK)**

Hire Your Attorney

Upon completion of the class, you should find an attorney at this point. Unless you have another resource, use the attorney from the first-time homebuyers class. Fees should range from $200-$400 per purchase transaction, which is normally a flat rate. You will need your attorney frequently once you begin shopping with the realtor and agreements begin to present themselves. There will be an agreement for representation from the realtor and then the purchase agreement for the prospective property. Many documents could follow the purchase

agreement, but there are several steps within the offer process through closing where your attorney and the sellers attorney will correspond. You will be directly involved in these matters so you'll learn from this experience. This will be your greatest lessons on how real estate transactions go. Pay attention and ask questions. **(TASK)**

Pre-Approval

After you have ensured that your credit report is accurate and done your best to raise your credit score, you are ready to apply. The next thing to do is to connect with a lender that supports the first-time homebuyer program of your choice. Here is an example of a website that tells you who the lenders are that support the first-time homebuyer program you're targeting.

Go to -

https://www.nerdwallet.com/blog/mortgages/first-time-home-buyer-programs-by-state/

When you go to the site above, it has a link for all the lenders that support the first-time homebuyer programs in that state. These are very conveniently prepared for you! Check it out!

Be sure to run this search for lenders in your area. **(TASK)** Lenders review all relevant documents to confirm you are qualified for the loan program you are pursuing. Your credit score is very important and must be at least 500 to qualify for specific federal loan programs.

These federal programs are for first-time homebuyers with low credit scores. If this fits your needs, seek this program out at the county you are planning to purchase your home in.

Below are the different federal loan programs and some are not specific to any first-time homebuyer programs:

- ✓ Veterans Affairs (VA) loan program, which doesn't set minimum credit scores, has zero down payment options and seeks a maximum 41 percent DTI (Debt to Income)
- ✓ The U.S. Department of Agriculture (USDA), which also has a zero down payment program in areas that fall into the USDA revitalization map.

The Federal Housing Administration (FHA), which is a popular choice among first-time homebuyers who do not have a lot of money for down payments and those that have bad credit.

- ▪ FHA requires a 3.5% down payment. Get your grant to take care of the down payment.
- ✓ Debt-to-income (DTI) also varies according to these programs.

Notice that the objective of these first-time homebuyer programs is to get you into a home. The programs cater to your circumstance. Although there is a program that supports you getting a home with a low credit score of 500 or above, you still need to prepare yourself to achieve a better credit rating for your future endeavors. There will be several instances in life where your credit will either help you more or help you less. Credit ratings can affect your ability to borrow funds. Borrowing funds is very essential in making advancements in your personal wealth. How you use the borrowed funds is the next important factor. Make getting your credit score to a healthy level a priority. A healthy level is at or above 680. Ideally, you want to target being over 720. Reference the direction on www.creditkarma.com for more details.

The lenders are to apply for any grant programs of your choice on your behalf. You should ask them about this when you call. Be specific about the program you plan to use. **(TASK)** Ensure the loan officer applying on your behalf has experience and is willing to secure the programs you're targeting. Down payment assistance programs must be well-secured before you attend the closing for your home. Otherwise, while you may qualify, you will miss out on the funds due to lack of preparation and planning. Don't let this happen! Grants must reach the stage of approval well before the closing on your new home!

Chapter 2 – Understanding the Grant System

Finding Grants

All grants can be defined as forgivable loans meeting the qualifying expectations during a prorated time period. First-time homeowner grants usually work in conjunction with low-down-payment mortgages. For instance, FHA mortgages generally require a 3.5% down payment of the purchase price of a home. There are also conventional mortgage programs that allow you to purchase a home with a 3% down payment. The percentages down are always relative to the purchase price of the home.

First-time homeowner grants are created to cover the down payment requirement. The combination of the grant with the first mortgage may allow you to purchase a home with a zero down payment. This is the objective of securing the grants. Still be prepared for the out of pocket expenses like home inspections, loan origination fees, attorney fee, earnest money and appraisal. These programs are for first-time homebuyers however, this definition oftentimes includes someone who has not owned a home in the past three years. Also, these grants are available for buying owner-occupied homes only. They are not available for buying a second home or investment property.Grants have limits. For instance, the actual dollar amount of the grant is usually capped at a certain percentage of the loan. Let's use an example where we acquire grant money to use toward the 3.5% down payment for a FHA loan.

If the down payment assistance limit is $7,000 or 3.5%, the maximum purchase price of a property by using a 96.5% first mortgage would be a $200,000 purchase price ($200,000 x .035 = $7,000). Most grants are available on a 5-year term and require that you live in the home for the five years in order for the assistance to be 100% forgiven. If you leave the residence early, the payment assistance is prorated on how much will be forgiven. For example, if you move out after 4 years, 4/5 or 80%, of the loan will be forgiven.

Income limits also matter when it comes to grants. The limits vary from county to county, and are generally based on the median household income in the area. For instance, grant availability may only apply to households who have annual incomes that are below the median. In most cases, grants are really loans that are potentially 100% forgivable.

After you've selected the lender you will partner with, it is important that you verify your programs of choice through the loan officer. This will take place before your pre-approval. Once, pre-approved, you can get the lender to start working towards securing the grants right away. Find and apply for as many grants as possible to meet the maximum allowable down payment assistance. You have nothing to lose by doing so.

Finding a Lender

The best mortgage lenders for first-time homebuyers prefer VA, FHA, and USDA loans. These loans have low minimum down payments and the USDA loan does not have any down payment at all. You should reference the information you were provided in the first time home buyers class that you will attend. There will also be a reference to the lenders that support the grant programs of your choice. When you contact the lenders, you will need to ask about the particular programs that you want because all the lenders listed don't necessarily support all the programs you may be interested in. **(TASK)** It is your responsibility to find the lender that supports the programs you want and then ensure their APR rates are competitive.

Simply call around to prospective banks that support the programs you want and ask each of them what their lowest APR rate is today for borrowers in the highest credit score bracket. **(TASK)** Whoever has the programs you need and has the lowest APR, that's your bank! Be sure their loan officer has secured several grants in the past. This is an important and cost savings step!

As a first-time homebuyer, shopping mortgage lenders will feel like a huge chore. But, similar to choosing an insurance policy or buying a car, if you take your time and apply due diligence, it will save you heartache, regrets, and money. Here are tips for finding a lender for your first mortgage:

✓ Know your credit score and history as lenders use these two bits of information to decide your mortgage interest rate and more.

✓ Investigate assistance programs as some state housing finance agencies and lenders can help with a down payment and closing costs.

✓ Seek out government loans: VA, FHA, and USDA loans generally offer more relaxed qualification requirements.

✓ Request quotes from different lenders: pay particular attention to the Annual Percentage Rate (APR) and any origination fees.

✓ Get pre-approved before you start shopping for houses: a preapproval letter is needed to help you stay on budget and also to tell sellers that you mean business.

Chapter 3 – Wise Choices

Intelligent Shopping

Mortgage brokers exist to assist you in borrowing funds and to answer the question of how much you can afford to borrow. If your budget only permits you to obtain a mortgage below $1,000 per month (including HOA or taxes) and total monthly expenses of $1,400, then you should avoid shopping for a house where your mortgage and total expenses will exceed $1,400. You are likely to qualify for 43% debt to income. Therefore you'd have to make $3,256 or more per month to qualify for $1,400 worth of debt. This $1,400 would also include your mortgage. Don't over extend yourself! Just because the bank doesn't count all specific debts you may be incurring, doesn't mean you sign up for more than you can handle. This means that the total of your entire debt payments and the mortgage should add up to 43% of your gross income.

If you decide to go over this amount, after making payment for other expenses like food, taxes, and dining out with friends and family, you may end up feeling "house poor." The rule of thumb is to try your best to keep your total housing cost below 30% of your gross income. The lower the debt you accrue, the better for you. Don't plan your finances and mortgage such that you will be "house poor" for the next thirty years.

There are a few exceptions to this rule. For instance, if you have large savings but lower income, it may be okay for you to have a slightly higher debt-to-income ratio. This is okay because you are still safe if you have cash readily available to pay off the mortgage at any time. The other exception concerns self-employed folks who usually look much poorer on paper than they really are. Depending on their corporate structure, self-employed people may have more tax break options available which means they may have more disposable income. This allows them to spend more on housing compared to others who are not self employed after all the tax deferments.

Rentability

If you purchased your home as an investment to generate income, then it is important to conduct a rentability analysis and an ROI (Return on Investment) analysis. The two main rules that apply to these analyses are the 1% rule and the 50% rule. There are also other factors to consider before investing in the rental market, but these will keep you on course.

1% Rule

The rent that is expected should be at least 1% of the purchase price. This is a fast way to assess the income potential of a rental market. If it's greater than 1%, you stand a high chance of being cash flow positive. However, not all purchases will make you a full 1%. The further you are from this number, the more you have to rely on the property value appreciation to close the gap.

50% Rule

This estimates that the expenses of a property (excluding mortgage) is 50% of the gross rent. This will account for Homeowner Association (HOA) fees, repairs, property taxes, insurance, unoccupied months/vacancies and other miscellaneous expenses. It also helps the budget for one-time expenses, such as a new HVAC unit or a new roof. Although such will not occur every year, there should still be an advanced budget raised for it.Run your own rentability analysis for the home you are considering. **(TASK)**

Overspending on Amenities or Upgrades

The best ROI (return on investment) largely depends on minimizing expenses while maximizing revenue. But first-time homebuyers rarely consider ROI upfront. The excitement of owning their own homes usually makes them over-project into how the property will appreciate in value, thereby justifying upgrades at the time of purchase. Although it may be true that the resale value will improve, there is no guarantee that it will increase in proportion to the purchase price. When buying your first home, focus on the big picture.

27

Ignore the fancy built-ins, custom cabinetry, and designer fixtures until you are certain you are in your forever home. A major component of determining value related to making upgrades in your home, is using comparable homes that have these competitive upgrades as well as the applicable use of the materials.

With the right consideration, your first home is an investment that can be used to create steady cash flow. Your home can be rented out, sold to make a down payment on your next home, used as collateral on another property and much more! Evaluate what you're buying to ensure your future in this property is an appreciating asset.

Finding a Realtor

The steps you have taken so far have led you to this one. Congratulations! You are now ready to start shopping, but you need to thoroughly explore your options. This requires that you find a realtor, tell them about your plans and progress thus far, and follow their suggestions about insurance agents, home inspectors, attorneys, feedback on amenities of the potential neighborhood, etc.

✓ When finding your realtor you can use a service like Homelight to help match you with a realtor. Go to www.homelight.com for reference. **(TASK)**

Realtors conduct a lot of your groundwork upfront by connecting with listing agents on your behalf to set up showings and to help negotiate your purchase. However, you need to first tell them about the first-time homebuyer programs that you have underway and what the lender is working on for you. If they know you are pre-approved, they will take you more seriously as it shows you have done your own due diligence. Be mindful, you can negotiate brokerage fees, so tell them if you will only pay 2.5% commission versus 3%. **(TASK)** You can decide whether you want to have your attorney review the agent agreement from the realtor first before signing it. If so, collect the agreement from the realtor and let them know you'll follow up with them after your attorney has reviewed it. Before signing, be mindful to check the amount of days that you will be under agreement with the realtor and be sure you all are a good personality match for each other. 90 days is usually the norm. Anytime longer than this could be extensive, but make your own judgement.

The most important consideration that a first-time homebuyer has when it comes to selecting a real estate agent is excellent market knowledge. This includes knowledge of market trends, schools, the community, available finance options, recreation, transportation, local economy and local ordinances.

Execution

Buying your own home is highly competitive as there are many people out for the same opportunity. You have to follow up with each party to ensure there is continuous progress within each process. Check on the loan officer on securing the available first-time homebuyer programs. Follow up weekly with your loan officer. **(TASK)** Negotiate the best offer price with the realtor. After the realtor has drafted the offer, ask the realtor to send the offer to your attorney for review. Once approved by your attorney, your attorney should comply with the realtor that we are good to submit your offer. **(TASK)**

Here Are The Steps And Possibilities In The Offer Stage:

The seller will 1) accept your offer, 2) make a counteroffer with one or more changes, or 3) reject the offer outright.

1) If the seller accepts your purchase offer, with both buyer and seller signing off, you're in contract to complete the purchase.

2) If the Seller Counteroffers

> They are accepting some or most of the terms, but proposing changes to the following:
>
> - Price -- If the seller wants more money than offered
> - Closing date or occupancy date – If the seller needs more   time to move out, or

- Home purchase contract contingencies – For example, if the seller doesn't want to wait for you to sell your current house or wants you to schedule the inspections more quickly.

✓ You can accept the seller's counteroffer, reject it, or present a counter counteroffer. The negotiations will continue until you reach an agreement on the deal.

✓ Once both buyer and seller sign off, you're in contract to complete the deal.

3) If the Seller Rejects Your Offer

✓ Unless you're in a bidding war with other buyers, or you've submitted an absurdly lowball offer, it's unlikely that the seller will just say "No." Actually,

✓ the seller doesn't have to get back to you at all, but your real estate agents will probably be in contact, so that you'll find out the seller's response.

✓ If you do get an outright rejection, your agent may be able to find out why. This will help you craft a stronger, more appealing offer next time you find a house you're interested in. With all paperwork, ensure you accurately and completely fill out any applications, documents or paperwork. However, when it comes to the inspection, be calm and self-assured if anything alarming is found. Ask for credits or repairs as needed. You will be able to renegotiate any concerns post inspection.

Stay in your price margin when looking at properties with your realtor. An unknown repair need may push a prospective property over your budget. Negotiate and stand firm. Don't upscale your buying potential with a higher-priced property than you cannot afford. Sometimes, buyers are tempted to adjust their standards with enticing properties that are not suitable for their financial plan. Find the best home that your money can afford. In order to accomplish this you have to do your homework on all the neighborhoods that are suitable for your purchase price. You deserve the best! Go for the best your money can afford! Be a smart shopper by knowing which areas are highly sought out due to being in ideal locations. These type of decisions will help secure the potential in your property appreciating and you earning equity.

Closing

Congratulations! Your next and final step before receiving the keys to your new home is attending the closing. It will feel very good seeing the forgivable loan funds on your mortgage documents. You qualified, you put in the work and you deserve it. You're a homeowner! Well done! Closing (also referred to as completion or settlement) is the final step in executing a real estate transaction. The closing date is set during the negotiation phase, and is usually 30 to 45 days after the offer is formally accepted. On the closing date, the ownership of the property is transferred to you.

The buyer receives the keys, and the seller receives payment for the home from the lender. From the amount credited to the seller, the closing agent subtracts money to pay off the existing mortgage and other transaction costs. Deeds, loan papers, and other documents are prepared, signed, and filed with local property record offices.

Congratulations, you are a home owner that just received forgivable loans or grants for your down payment requirement! Nice job!! Not everyone has done it, so consider yourself as doing a job well done!

As a bonus for shopping with us, here is a reference list to several grant programs and their descriptions. Check for these or similar programs in your state. Search online for the "Your State" Home Buyers Grant and Resource Directory. Each state search will yield different results. Some may link to www.HUD.gov , some will yield the state PDF directory and some will be apart of the nonprofit literature. Please seek it out. The search will not directly place you to the manual, but is very directional. The following particular grant programs are from the Pennsylvania Grant and Resource Directory as examples.

Access Down Payment & Closing Cost Assistance – Homebuyers receiving funds through the Access Home Modification Program may also receive down payment/closing cost assistance through the Access Down Payment & Closing Cost Assistance Loan Program. Eligible homebuyers may receive between $1,000 and $15,000 in the form of a non-interest-bearing loan with no monthly payments. These assistance funds become due and payable upon the sale, transfer, or if the homebuyer fails to occupy the home as their primary residence. The household income limit for the program is set at 80 percent of the statewide median income. Notice that one loan is forgivable and one isn't.

HOMEstead Down payment and Closing Cost Assistance Loan – First-time homebuyers applying for a Keystone Home Loan and who also meet the income and purchase price limits of the HOMEstead program may qualify for $1,000 to $10,000 in down payment and closing cost assistance in the form of a no-interest, second mortgage loan. HOMEstead assistance funds are forgiven at 20 percent per year over five years. Income limits for the HOMEstead program are at or below 80 percent of the county's median income.

On the next page is a summary task list to help align your events. Good luck and I hope your first home purchase is a great experience!

Securing Grant Money: Step-by-Step Guide For First-Time Homebuyers Summary Task List				
Chapter 1	**Task 1**	**Task 2**	**Task 3**	**Task 4**
Stability	Verify emergency savings	Take time to compute and track all your expenses	Compute your transportation costs from potential new residential area	NONE
Motivation	NONE	NONE	NONE	NONE
Credit	Pull your credit report to verify accuracy. Dispute inaccuracies as needed.	Go to www.creditkarma.com to review and possibly open a free account	NONE	NONE
Eligibility	Gather your two most recent pay-stubs, three months of bank statements and two years of tax returns	Call a local lender and ask what their qualifying debt-to-income ratio is.	Confirm income eligibility and find a class in the county you are planning to purchase in.	Confirm the class issues the certificate
Hire An Attorney	Hire an Attorney	NONE	NONE	NONE
Pre-Approval	Locate the lenders that support the grant programs you are seeking in your area	Speak with the lender or loan officer to confirm they are familiar and have applied for the grants you are seeking	NONE	NONE
Chapter 2	**Task 1**	**Task 2**	**Task 3**	**Task 4**
Finding Grants	NONE	NONE	NONE	NONE

Finding a Lender	Ensure the lender has the grant programs you're looking for.	Ask the lender about the most competitive APR rates. Shop for the lender with the grants you need and lowest APR. Choose lender accordingly		
Chapter 3	**Task 1**	**Task 2**	**Task 3**	**Task 4**
Intelligent Shopping	NONE	NONE	NONE	NONE
Rentability	Run rentability analysis.			
Finding a Realtor	Find a realtor and inform them of your due diligence thus far and your goal.	Negotiate your commission costs.	NONE	NONE
Execution	Follow up weekly with the loan officer regarding the completion (and awarding) of your grant funds.	Send your purchase agreement to your attorney prior to submitting to the sellers agent.	NONE	NONE
Closing	NONE	NONE	NONE	NONE

This literature is brought to you by C.R. Wesley. Please rate this literature online provided the vendor has a review feature. We would appreciate your feedback and supportive rating if you found this book helpful. Thank you and keep striving for growth.

See more of our literature in our Real Estate Knowledge Series by C.R. Wesley below.

We strive to give you the tools to educate you and lead you to greater success.

- Securing Grant Money– Step-by-Step Guide for First-Time Homebuyers by C.R. Wesley
- Acquiring Rental Property – Learning Your Options in Starting Your Investment Portfolio by C.R. Wesley
- Understanding Tax Lien Investments – No Fluff by C.R. Wesley
- Understanding Tax Deed Investments – No Fluff by C.R. Wesley
- Buying and Selling Investments – Real Estate and Stock Market Guide by C.R. Wesley

ABOUT THE AUTHOR

Hello and thank you for selecting us as a resource. I sincerely hope that it was helpful for you and has provided value to you and your current situation. My ambition is to provide knowledge to help you build success through self-development and education. There is knowledge, but knowledge means little without action. My intention is to provide the knowledge and give you actionable steps that you can implement into your life. My contribution will not be about me, but more about the information and how to use it. I will try to be concise and engaging while also keeping the information compact. "Small" for convenience, but impactful is the goal.

Some people have a diverse knowledge of these topics and others do not. I intend to help more of us have the common knowledge of material that will help make your life healthier. Much our health starts in the mind. I intend to provide many materials that are all applicable in your self-growth. The applications of growth cover a wide variety.

My knowledge has started with extreme passion to be successful which transformed its way into my corporate atmosphere and I morphed the two. Through self-education; enabling me to initiate conversations, and continue growth through interaction and continued education, I was able to grow myself tremendously over time. Real Estate, Stock market, entrepreneurship, personal growth and leadership growth has been my experience.

My passion has always been for people and providing a means of growth for someone else. Hopefully, I can provide something inspirational, motivating and impactful. Myself always being "a sponge" of everything (in my atmosphere), I hope that I can drip positive elements on others and have them absorb it. For some it will be a drip and for others it will be a waterfall. I will try to accommodate both so everyone walks away with fruitful knowledge. I only ask that you pass on the positivity and healthy lifestyles to another.

Thank you for your time. C.R. Wesley.

Thanks for reading! Please add a short review on Amazon

and let me know what you thought!